July 2, 2003

To Lonie:

With all Best Wishes!

[illegible signature]

Recollections in Verse

Recollections in Verse

Leo J. Molner

VANTAGE PRESS
New York

FIRST EDITION

Published by Vantage Press, Inc.
516 West 34th Street, New York, New York 10001

Manufactured in the United States of America
ISBN: 0-533-11291-5

Library of Congress Catalog Card No.: 94-90627

0 9 8 7 6 5 4 3 2 1

I dedicate this book to everyone who enjoys poetry

Contents

Recollections in Verse

Old 5038

Each summer's morn, so long ago,
With Uncle Frank in back,
Old Junie and I begged to go
To see the railroad track.

We ran along the old town streets,
No reason now to fret,
But then we saw the railroad yard
And stopped to catch our breath.

We sat on rails to bide our time
And Frank would roll his own.
He gave us each a couple butts,
The first I've ever known.

I choked a lot the first few times.
They sure did burn my mouth.
No manly thing to do, but still,
I threw the buggers out.

We waited for the trains to come,
They looked so big and fast.
We looked inside the boxcars, too,
Our patience had to last.

Sometimes a freight train lumbered by,
As time was getting late.
But nothing matched the thrill to see
Old Fifty Thirty-eight.

Then suddenly the bells would ring,
The lighted gates came down.
Excitement rained all over us.
We screamed and danced around.

We strained our eyes to see the train
Come moving 'round the bend.
We waited such a long, long time;
It might not ever end.

At last, it came into our view,
Black smoke poured out its stack.
A big black engine, four-six-two
With nine long cars in back.

The whistle blew, the bell did clang,
White steam shot from each side.
We felt so scared, we ran a ways
And felt the urge to hide.

As it passed by, the fireman waved,
While shov'ling in the coal.
We saw the fire inside the cab.
The noise just shook your soul.

The people in the cars were dressed
And looked so dignified.
The train roared by and down the track.
Our joys were satisfied.

316

As five year olds, we were impressed,
"Our mighty special train!"
We often wondered where it went,
Like Boston, France, or Spain.

While other trains did pass by too,
But none of them as great,
As the golden numbers on the cab . . .
Of Fifty Thirty-eight.

The Ospreys

The osprey circled in the sky
And surveyed its domain.
It checked the pole, the nest, the perch,
The reasons why it came.

It circled even wider still,
I'm sure it checked the sea.
It soared above the beach, the park
As far as I could see.

At last it landed on its perch
And checked the homestead out.
The nest was still there, just the same,
As when they headed south.

That place was home to it, I'm sure,
It raised a fam'ly there.
It seems like only weeks ago,
They were a happy pair.

The osprey stood on watch for days,
A lonely figure, true.
It chirped almost the whole day long.
It searched the whole sky blue.

But then, one day, I looked out back
And to my great surprise,
One in the nest, one on the perch
Two ospreys, what a prize!

There followed many days and weeks
Of waiting for the sign,
When newborn babies did arrive
And feeding was on time.

An awful frenzy did ensue,
Three chicks came through alive.
While growing bigger with each day,
They all began to thrive.

The parents struggled through each day.
They flew off many times.
In search of fish to feed their young
They brought back many kinds.

The chicks grew bolder with each day
They scampered 'round the nest.
They chirped a lot and stretched their wings
To see which one was best.

The parents doted on their young
Through driving rain or sun.
Sometimes I worried for their care
The ospreys always won.

The nest is perched on top a pole.
A pond is just below.
A heavy traffic road is near
And condos 'round the pole.

Somehow the ospreys manage this.
They never seem to care.
They simply flap their great big wings
And soar up in the air.

Then one sad day, the noise will end.
The chirping will be gone.
The ospreys will all fly away
Their absence won't be long.

I'll look around again next year,
And search the whole sky blue.
For that solitary osprey
Coming back to me and you.

Footprints in the Sand

While walking on the beach one day,
Without a thing to do,
The breeze was light, the water warm.
The sky was azure blue.

The sea gulls soared above the shore.
Large boats were out to sea.
And I was real contented there,
It felt just great to be.

And as I walked there, so serene,
Without a care at hand,
I looked around and saw a pair
Of footprints in the sand.

They looked so solitary there.
No other tracks in sight.
I pondered when they were put there,
This morning or last night.

I wondered where this person was,
Who left his tracks behind.
Could he be just ahead of me?
Would he be hard to find?

What kind of person would he be?
What name did he go by?
How old was he, what color hair,
And would he laugh or cry?

This person surely had a job.
I hope he had a home.
What kind of family did he have
Or did he live alone?

I wondered where these tracks would lead
To good or maybe bad?
I hope that he finds happiness
The best that can be had.

Whenever I go walking now
I hope you understand.
I always stop and look around
For footprints in the sand.

The Boy I Used to Be

Of all the problems I have faced
There is one thing I know:
That childhood ends so very fast.
I wish it were not so.

I do remember being young
And all those little things.
The highs and lows of growing up,
The joys it often brings.

I played the games that children do,
I always knew the score.
Sometimes I missed the golden ring
But always tried once more.

When first I swung a baseball bat
I hit the ball so far.
It shot right up into the air
And hit the neighbor's car.

Just one of many lessons learned
A time of growing up.
New friends were made most every day
Adventures filled the cup.

The time when I discovered girls
It was a sight to see.
I did not know just what to say.
She looked so sweet to me.

I wonder where she is today
And what she may look like?
And do her eyes still sparkle so,
As when she rode my bike?

For when I think of childhood friends,
I see them as before,
All young and fresh with youthful smiles
And happy to the core.

No sign of age upon their brows
The future yet to come.
I hope that life was good to them
God bless them, every one.

The years just passed by in a blur.
I'm sure they took their toll.
I wonder where these people are
And how they played their role.

But, most of all, I think of me
And how I aged so fast.
My mind still harbors many things,
By now, the distant past.

But when I look into the glass,
An old man looks at me.
I wonder then what happened to
The boy I used to be.

Morning Glories

While walking on the beach today,
I came upon a place,
That looked so wild and natural
I quickly slowed my pace.

I finally stopped to look around
And saw some rocks and grass.
The sea oats were all swaying there,
The water looked like glass.

White clouds had billowed in the sky
And softly hugged the land,
While purple morning glories grew
And blossomed in the sand.

I wondered how they prospered there,
No nourishment to see.
They must have struggled to maintain
This beauty, just for me.

Mother

A mom must be so many things
To children in her care.
From early days to grown-up years,
Her love is always there.

So often in the wee small hours
When sickness makes its call,
And cries and sobs just fill the air,
Dear mom will fix it all.

She'll be right there through tummy aches,
Through bruises, scrapes, and falls.
And when the darkness scares you so,
She'll light the darkest halls.

But when you're hungry, best of all,
She'll know just what you need.
She'll heat your milk and warm your food
And feed you, yes indeed.

She'll mend your clothes and buy you toys,
Appease you when you cry.
She'll comb your hair and wash your hands
And keep your bottom dry.

Her love will see you through travails.
She'll know what's best for you.
A hug and squeeze will mean so much,
When you are feeling blue.

Then when you grow so big and strong,
Become an adult, too,
Have children all your very own
She'll show you what to do.

She'll nourish them, as she did you
And help to light the way.
She'll hold them, squeeze them, all day long
And love them every day.

For mothers are a special kind
Of person on this earth,
Who never seem to tire of God's
Great miracle of birth.

Friendship

What is a friend? I heard them say,
So many years ago.
I thought about it many times
Then said, I did not know.

Maybe a buddy is a friend.
So surely is a pal.
A crony seems to fit the bill,
Companion beats them all.

Associate is businesslike.
A colleague sounds so cool.
Accomplice sounds so criminal.
Confederate does too.

A friendship may be all these things
But something's lacking still.
I think that what I'm looking for
Is really hard to fill.

To have one, must you be a friend?
Or can it be one way?
Must there be limitations set?
Or only all the way!

Can friendship stay forever true,
Or must it sadly die?
I hope it lasts a long, long time
Not eight o'clock to five.

I think that I would like a friend
To stay through thick and thin,
And share my life's experience
And let the sunshine in.

A smile or two from day to day
Would help an awful lot.
Especially on those days when
The going gets so hot.

I think, I'd like my friend to be
A very gentle soul,
Someone who would have faith in me
And play a major role.

Someone to help me find the way
And aid me when I fall.
Someone to put up with my faults
And stay when others call.

And if I need a helping hand,
I hope it's there for me.
And if good fortune comes my way
I want him there to see.

For I would share my earthly goods
With such a treasured friend.
I'd help him on life's journey, too,
Down to the very end.

So if you have a real friend,
It's better than the gold,
That people gather all their lives,
But have no friend . . . when old.

The *Bonhomme Richard*

One evening in September,
In seventeen seventy-nine,
Four gallant ships came sailing through
The mist and swirling brine.

They sailed along the English coast
And raised some havoc there;
The Colonies' first navy fleet
Was really on a tear.

Then suddenly they came upon
The English Baltic fleet
Returning from their ports of call.
A real commercial feat.

They had two ships protecting them;
A sloop of war was there
And H.M.S. *Serapis*, too,
With fifty guns to spare.

The English ships were sleek and fast
Not eager to take flight.
The other ships were old and slow
But spoiling for a fight.

Bonhomme Richard then fired a shot,
Just when the sun had set.
A starboard, broadside shot that made
The naval battle threat.

The ships then came about to fight
And shot some volleys out.
Great damage to the ships occurred.
They turned and came about.

The blood ran heavy o'er the decks,
The bodies piling up.
The fires were burning so intense,
The masts were cracking up.

The stern of the *Serapis* then
Was rammed by the *Richard*
Close quarters fighting then ensued
They fought so long and hard.

"Has your ship struck?" the captain asked.
And John Paul Jones replied,
"I have not yet begun to fight!"
Those words he would abide.

The battle being thus begun,
It lasted through the night
With unrelenting fury 'til
The early morning light.

With grappling hooks and musket fire
The carnage was immense.
The wooden ships were smashed with holes;
The fire was so intense.

A truce was called to fight the fires.
And when they were put out,
The battle then commenced once more.
The end was still in doubt.

The spectators watched all night long.
The fires lit up the sky
From chalky cliffs, Flamborough Head.
They watched the brave men die.

At last the Captain gave his sword
The English had enough.
The Colonists had won the fight
The costs were oh, so tough.

The old *Richard* would sink that day.
It gave a mighty fight.
The famous words of John Paul Jones
Would lead our nation's might.

Just Passing By

I saw her walking in the surf.
Just slowly passing by.
She strolled awhile and stopped awhile,
Enough to catch my eye.

She wore a pretty bathing suit.
Her skin was sunburned red.
I think she was from somewhere else;
That's what her actions said.

She stooped to pick up little shells
A bag was at her side.
The sunlight shone upon her face
Her smile was magnified.

For one long moment our eyes met
It lasted quite awhile.
She then continued on her quest,
I watched for half a mile.

These special moments stay with me
As I sit in the sand
And watch the people walking through
This sun-drenched fairyland.

Butterflies

It seems to me, that in my youth
My life was simpler than today.
And nature was more bountiful
In almost every special way.

I do recall the birds that sang
And how they flew from tree to tree.
Their songs were so melodious.
Their beauty meant so much to me.

And butterflies flew to and fro
Among the flowers in the beds.
A mass of white and golden ones,
They hovered o'er our bobbing heads.

The kingly Monarch butterflies,
With many colors on their wings,
Would fly about for us to see.
I surely miss those little things.

And if you stood and tried to catch
A little one, or maybe two,
To my delight and great surprise,
A great big one would land on you.

I wonder how, in this great land,
Where birds still fly and sing their song,
Where flowers grow and streams are high,
But . . . where have all the butterflies gone?

My Friend Snowy

Old Snowy came again today
And made her usual rounds.
She walked right up to my back door
And made some birdlike sounds.

She stared at me and danced a bit,
Then shook her perky head.
I waved to her and said, "Just wait!"
She wanted to be fed.

This egret has a yellow beak.
Her legs are long and black.
Her feathers are so snowy white.
They cover front and back.

I mostly give her meat to eat.
She'll take most anything.
She has a lot of patience, though.
She'll wait for what I bring.

She often disappears for days,
Then suddenly comes back,
And acts as though she owns the place
Just looking for a snack.

It's kind of nice to see her there,
She looks so stern and bold.
She chases other birds away,
This is her space, I'm told.

One day she walked right in my house.
I scooted her away.
I know some day she won't come back;
A real unhappy day.

Batter Up

His baseball glove was old and worn.
He oiled it just today.
A ball of cord was wrapped in tape,
But it would last the day.

Unless it fell in Groffski's yard,
Who always kept the ball.
He loved to see you sweat and squirm.
A tough bird, all in all.

Or if it fell on Joe's garage,
You had to get the ball.
And if your climbing skills were bad,
"Three Outs!" was then the call.

He wondered who he'd be today?
Ted Williams was a cinch,
Or maybe Jolting Joe was nice,
Bob Feller, if he pitched.

As one by one, the players came,
He hoped they'd have enough.
At least one game, he'd like to play.
That shouldn't be too tough.

They found some bases in the scrap,
The best one was home plate.
A bat was tossed to choose up sides,
The time was getting late.

The little field was tidied up.
The boys were all in place.
He stepped right up and waved the bat,
The first pitch, he would face.

The ball was coming o'er the plate.
He swung the bat real hard.
He hit the ball so high and far . . .
It fell, in Groffski's yard.

The Man on the Beach

I saw a man down on the beach,
He seemed to come my way.
I couldn't see him very well,
It was the end of day.

He walked along the drifting sand,
His feet were bare, you see.
Still closer came this bearded man,
His path now, straight to me.

It seemed to be a long, long time
Before our two eyes met.
I felt him look into my soul,
So strange, I can't forget.

I know he searched the years I've spent
Upon this earthly plane.
He found the good and bad I did . . .
The joys, the hurt, the pain.

I wondered why he looked in me,
This man down by the sea.
I still had many things to do,
Before I could be free.

With obligations yet to meet,
I pondered what to say.
I thought that he might talk to me
And maybe show the way.

He finally turned and walked away,
His footprints in the sand.
I heard a voice say, "Do not fear,
You'll always have my hand."

The Cookie Jar

With big blue eyes, he looked at me
And said it wasn't so.
He didn't break the cookie jar.
It fell down, don't you know?

The chair was still there, near the shelf,
Some books on top of it.
The glass and cookies on the floor.
I almost had a fit.

I looked at Josh and he was scared.
Big tears welled in his eyes.
I did not know just what to say.
His story was a prize.

At three years old, I was amazed
That he could climb so high.
He surely had a lot of nerve
To give it such a try.

I placed the chair where it belonged,
And swept the pieces up.
He cried so hard, I had to stop
And pick old Joshua up.

We talked awhile and laughed awhile
And found some cookies, too.
Next time he wants something, I'm sure,
He'll ask me what to do.

Morning on the Beach

The sun was rising in the east.
It barely cleared the trees.
The wind was blowing from the west,
A soft and gentle breeze.

I walked along the lovely beach,
Just taking in the sights,
And passed by people hunting shells,
Some youngsters flying kites.

The rolling waves came into shore
And surged up on the beach,
While sand crabs scampered in their holes
As far as they could reach.

And sandpipers, in unison,
Moved left and then to right;
Their movement was so magical
It was a pretty sight.

They searched for critters in the sand
Until the surf approached.
Then turned and briskly walked away
As though they all were coached.

Giant tracks of loggerheads were there.
They lay their eggs at night.
The turtles then go back to sea,
Before the morning light.

And pelicans stood on the dock.
They'd sit and wait and look
For fishermen to catch a fish,
Then dive and clean his hook.

With seagulls screeching overhead
And egrets, tall and grand,
The beach is such an awesome place,
A kingdom in the sand.

Springtime

The winter's fled the land once more
And left the scene quite bare.
For where the snow and ice prevailed,
The mud is thickest there.

But I did see, not far from here,
In majesty supreme,
Amid the mire and scrawny weeds
A blade of grass, bright green.

The winding brook is deeper too,
As fish jump high and free,
And tiny children fly their kites,
While shouting happily.

The skies in spring, like pale blue eyes,
Are something nice to see.
Especi'ly trimmed with silver clouds
Above a roaring sea.

And, if you listen now, you'll hear
The robins' song of cheer,
Announcing spring to one and all,
The best time of the year.

Winter Storm

The wind came roaring o'er the hill
And down the other side,
While bending trees bereft of leaves
And gave them quite a ride.

The roar was so extremely loud
Just like unearthly moans.
The cold was piercing like a sword.
It chilled your very bones.

White snow came biting at your face
And stung your cold bare hands.
It soon became so hard to see,
Not much like fairylands.

It seemed like only yesterday,
The trees were mauve and gold
And leaves were gently falling down,
The days were getting cold.

Some leaves just landed on the ground
And gathered on the grass,
While others held on to the end.
Each one tried hard to last.

Some leaves fell in the nearby brook
And sailed away downstream.
The current took them quite a ways
They all fulfilled a dream.

Some bobbed and weaved in waters rough,
Some sailed on even keel.
A few got shipwrecked on the banks,
Some hit the water wheel.

Those days are gone away I'm sure
For winter's claimed the land.
'Til spring shows up again next year
The skies are gray and bland.

But, now the wind is dying down
And peace is in the air.
For where the snow and ice hit hard
There is a softness there.

Large flakes are falling from the sky
And slowly sail around.
The trees are covered all in white,
A blanket on the ground.

The snow will last a little while
Then slowly disappear.
Until we see the next snowfall
I'm sure we'll all be here.

Thanksgiving

The days are shorter than they were.
The chestnut trees are bare,
But nestled 'neath the stalks of corn,
A pumpkin lies with care.

And up on high, the snowflakes dance
As on the wind they ride.
While hobbled in the great red barn
A turkey stands with pride.

Within the house, the children play
In scent of mincemeat pies.
As blushing berries, cheek to cheek,
Look up with twinkling eyes.

For coming soon, a day of thanks,
When people gather 'round
To offer up a silent prayer
In gratitude profound.

Christmas Time

Boys and girls all shout with glee
Dancing 'round the Christmas tree.
Talking, laughing, singing rhyme,
Gee, there's fun at Christmas time.

Berries placed in holly wreaths,
Fruits and toys and candy treats,
Shining stars and mistletoe,
Even strangers say, "Hello!"

Sleigh rides, skating, big snow fights,
Anything your heart delights.
Children have one thing to fear:
Christmas comes just once a year.

The Chosen Tree

A lonely pine upon a hill
So far away from strife,
Stood tall and straight and very green
In snow so soft and white.

Its roots grew deep in friendly soil.
With pride it did abound.
Then one sad day, two woodsmen came
And severed tree and ground.

They carried it for miles and miles
And laughed along the way.
Then placed it in a great big room
Where children loved to play.

They dressed it up in fine array
Of tinsel lights and stars,
And under branches, gifts were laid
Like trains and dolls and cars.

Once more the mountain pine was proud
As children danced with glee,
While shouting season's greetings
Around the Christmas tree.

Buffy

Old Buffy ate a bug today.
He didn't even gag.
He licked his chops a little bit,
That little Scalawag.

He ran, he pranced around the yard,
Then jumped a little fence,
Then bounded high into my lap
So full of confidence.

I scolded him a long, long time.
'Not nice to eat a bug!
His big brown eyes just looked at me.
I had to give a hug.

We really are great friends, you see,
He's always lots of fun.
But every now and then . . . Oh, Oh!
He ate another one!

The Road

The night descendeth on my soul.
Life's path I cannot see.
A beacon please, to light my way!
A candle pray . . . for me?

How can I fare in darkest night?
How many secrets solve?
One thousand problems I must meet,
And untold trials resolve.

A shaft of light is all I beg
To better let me see
The road upon which I journey,
A ray of hope . . . for me?

Retirement Day

At last, this is the final day.
It's time to move along.
For since I had the paper route,
I worked for this so long.

I toiled on many kinds of jobs
And learned along the way.
I tried to do the best I could
On each and every day.

I kept my mind on earning pay.
Some goals, I had to set.
I tried to climb the ladder up,
As far as I could get.

I tried to help my friends at work.
I taught them all I knew.
And if I did some good each day
I felt successful, too.

For me, the time is here at last
To do the things I planned,
To set my sights on other goals
And let my life expand.

But now, it's time for me to go.
I say, "Farewell!" to you.
I hope your future's awfully good
In everything you do.

Summer Storm

It's dark and dreary now,
A mist is everywhere,
But dancing shadows shriek
Within the woodland there.

The leaves begin to dance
And move about in glee,
While rain begins to fall
So softly, at my feet.

Now light'ning rends the sky
And reaches for the ground,
While the thunder, thunder,
Thunder crashes around.

The soft and gentle rain
Arises from its sleep
To bite and sting your face
So savagely, so deep.

The winds begin to roar
And freeze your shaking bones,
Then slowly whine and cry
In such unearthly moans.

Then quick as it arrived
So cruelly intent,
To rack nature's garden
With a great force unmeant.

The sun shines undaunted
Upon the land and sea,
Which opens your heart wide,
And makes you glad to be.

Purpose

Oh, can it be,
That this is me
So broken and forlorn?

If I could see
The wisdom tree
To learn why I was born.

For if I go
And get to know
My purpose in this life.

I could then show
A heart aglow
With vigor for this strife.

Someone Else's Shadow

I wonder how my life would be
If I would have to follow
And do my daily services,
In someone else's shadow.

How hopeless it must be to work
And strive along life's highway,
Without a chance to show that you
Could do the best job your way.

But, you can shed the darkness there
By lighting your own candle,
And let the world come looking in,
To see what you can handle.

How nice it is to use your skills
Around life's pain and sorrow.
Out in the sun and bright blue sky
With no one's name to borrow.

To never have a chance at all
Is such an old, old story.
You've got to show what you can do
Then savor your own glory.

You've got to be to yourself true.
You must depend on nothing.
If you expect to persevere,
Your hard work must be shining.

For no one lights the way for you,
They'll always say, "Tomorrow!"
And let you find your lonely way
In someone else's shadow.

Death

Hark! What is there?
In the corner there,
By the opening of the door.
It starts and moves,
Which certainly proves
It is I it's looking for.

A face appears
And sadly jeers
At I, the chosen one.
It looks like he,
But can it be,
That which humans shun?

He whispers, "Come!"
This lowly one,
Then reaching out his hand.
He bids me time
To sip the wine
Of this enchanted land.

No one escapes
His dreadful cape
Of sweet inviting scent.
It surely pays
To mend your ways,
To pray, and then repent.

For at this hour
You sum your power,
To cushion your last breath.
And then you talk
And slowly walk,
Hand in hand, with Death.

Orgy in a Graveyard

Once I walked a lonely path
A lonely, lonely, lonely path.
The moon was dark, as dark as that
Beneath the folds of my cravat.
As I walked, I roughly stumbled
And of course, cursedly mumbled,
For you see I almost tumbled,
Tumbled headlong into that.

Instantly, a noise I heard.
The flutter of an ancient bird
With eyes that caused my blood to curd,
It hovered o'er the brink of that.
Distant bells began their tolling,
Showing plainly never knowing
Of the shadows ever strolling
Round and round the edge of that.

Then I struggled to my feet.
Intent to force myself to seek
A haven free from those who creep
And crawl about in fits of wrath.
Still the demons came much nearer.
Dancing shadows in a mirror.
Always darker, never clearer
Edging closer yet to that.

Suddenly the world did turn.
Imprisoned in a spinning urn
While plants and shrubs and trees did burn,
I fell into the midst of that.
Flashing, flashing, thunder crashing!
Savage teeth of beasts came gnashing.
Brutal fiends with fingers slashing
Far inside the depths of that.

"Beasts! Oh, Beasts! Begone!" I said.
"Ye ugly Ghouls, who feast on dead."

Alleys

Whatever happened to alleys?
Alleys had garages, trash cans,
Telephone poles with wires.
Most were paved.
Lots of things happened in alleys.
People washed their cars,
Trash was picked up.
And kids played in alleys.
It was kind of the neighborhood playground.
A lot of baseball was played there.
So was dock on the rock and kick the can.
Some played catch.
Others just played.
Most kids tried jamming Pet Milk cans on their heels
And ran around like horses.
Some kids skated.
Alleys were like streets,
Only friendlier.

Games Unplayed

What kind of games do kids play now?
What ever happened to "It"?
Also called "Tag."
Do kids play jump rope anymore?
Do they know what a rope is?
How about kick the can,
Or hopscotch?
Do they play release the Belgian,
Or dock on the rock?
Skates are in vogue,
But are skateboards?
Where is the ingenuity,
That young minds had?
Has anyone heard of kazoos
Or ocarinas?
Do kids whistle anymore?
Do they skip?
Do they know how?
Has anyone heard a harmonica lately?
On a front porch?
What happened to front porches?
Whatever happened to kids?
They're hanging around
At the malls.

You

You are to me the summer sky,
A silver brook and trout that fly.
You are to me a rose of red
That's nestled in a flower bed.

You are to me a bird that sings,
The rainbow that a shower brings.
Your gentle smile, your twinkling eyes,
Which light the night, like fireflies.

You are the universe to me.
The sun, the moon, the land, the sea.
You are to me the grass, the trees,
The early morning summer breeze.

You are to me so wonderful
And yet so softly beautiful.
And when your tiny hands touch me
I feel my worries all set free.

You are to me the answered prayer.
The knowing that you're always there.
And if I left out anything . . .
You are to me just . . . everything.

The Golden Years

I met a lonely man one day
Who looked so sad and blue.
He sat there looking so forlorn.
I knew not what to do.

He didn't seem to want to talk,
No single word to say.
His time was spent in reverie,
With thoughts of yesterday.

I lingered there a little while;
I thought he'd like to talk.
I really tried to draw him out.
Alas, I took a walk.

I didn't see him for a while.
I thought he moved away.
I wondered what became of him
He disappeared, they say.

Then to my great surprise, one day,
I saw him once again.
He had a smile upon his face—
The happiest of men.

He looked at me with such a grin,
And told me what transpired.
He said he worked a long, long time,
And finally retired.

He didn't plan his golden years.
That fact was oh, so true.
He spent his days just wasting time,
Without a thing to do.

He said that he found happiness
When once he understood,
A lot of time is wasted time
Unless you do some good.

He said that now he spends his time
Just helping those he can;
No greater calling is there than
To help your fellow man.

Gettysburg

The mighty Blue and Gray came down
To Gettysburg one day.
The year was eighteen sixty-three;
They skirmished right away.

The next day was July the first—
An awful day, 'tis true—
The armies had all gathered there;
A battle would ensue.

The Gray came in from north and west;
They fought their way through town.
The dogged men in blue drew back,
Their world turned upside down.

On Ridge and Cemetery Hills
And Culps Hill to the right,
The Northern troops had gathered there
To dig in for the fight.

One hundred fifty thousand troops
Were poised to start the fray.
July the second came at last;
There would be hell to pay.

The Northern generals were there,
George Meade and Buford, too.
The South had Pickett, Longstreet, Lee,
And Armistead there, too.

The South attacked the Northern flanks—
T'was late that afternoon.
The fighting fierce, the losses high,
The North repulsed them soon.

Then Meade had checked the battlefield,
He had a plan to fill;
He thought the South would charge right up
To Cemetery Hill.

He moved his cannon to the hill,
His center line was weak.
The clump of trees would be their goal,
"More troopers to the peak!"

The next day was July the third.
The day was just so fine.
From woods on Seminary Ridge
There came a long gray line.

The men in gray stood bravely there
With bayonets held high.
The finest army of the South
Would give the battle cry.

Then Armistead, with hat on sword,
His white head in the breeze,
Said, "Forward, guide and center, March!"
Moved toward the clump of trees.

One mile away the march began,
All thirteen thousand strong,
And Pickett galloped to the front,
In center of the throng.

The North was stunned at such a sight;
The men moved in a row,
The drummers drummed, red flags unfurled—
Such gallantry on show.

The Northern cannon then laid down;
A deadly rain of fire.
They blasted holes along the line.
The South would not retire.

As one man fell, another ran
And took his comrade's place.
On up the slope, at doubletime,
To battle face to face.

The Northern rifles, firing now,
The Rebels reached the wall.
In smoke and fire and blood and cries,
The Southern colors fall.

The musket fire was so intense
Men fell to left and right.
Both sides would pay a heavy cost
For this immortal fight.

Then Pickett's Charge was doomed to fail
When he himself went down.
The Southern troops lost half their men;
They had to turn around.

When Lee had seen the battle costs,
He said it was his fault.
For Longstreet stood, the night before,
Against this feared assault.

Lee gathered up his weary men
And slowly pulled away.
Meade's troops pursued them without heart.
The North had saved the day.

Some say this battle turned the tide;
Some say it was not so.
There were so many battles fought,
But many more to go.

The Marina

The sea gulls soared up in the sky
And watched the people passing by.
Sunbathers stretched out on the sand,
While fleecy clouds caressed the land.

Brown pelicans sat on the dock
And patiently ignored the clock.
They first appeared just after noon;
The fishing boats would be there soon.

When all the boats arrived at five
The fishing docks all came alive.
The people scurried here and there
With strings of fish just everywhere.

The catch for many was so fine;
A few there had an empty line.
Large fish were hung up just for show;
They tempted you to want to go.

And when they cleaned the fish on board,
The pelicans and sea gulls soared.
They dove and fought for food that way.
The fishing fleet sails every day.

Missing You

I think of you at dawn's first light,
As I awake each day.
And all day long, I think of you,
Although you're far away.

I see your face in every crowd;
I always look again.
I'm disappointed all the time,
I miss you so, right then.

Sometimes I'm in a crowded room.
A movement taunts my eye.
I feel it's you; it must be you!
But once again, I sigh.

At night my dreams are all of you;
I hold you close to me.
I never want to let you go.
You mean so much, you see.

I miss you so, you'll never know,
The pain that's in my heart.
I only hope that someday soon
We'll meet and never part.

Dreams of Yesteryear

The railroad tracks are rusty now
They dream of yesteryear.
Where are the trains, which plied these rails?
Why did they disappear?

Where did the gangs, who worked the tracks,
Those gandy-dancers, go?
With ten-pound hammers, spikes, and tongs,
They made the railroads grow.

Steam engines ruled the right-of-ways
With tenders, boxcars, too.
Cabooses, flatcars, all in line;
The brakemen waved at you.

And just on time the Eight-Fifteen
Would highball down the track.
We'd sit and wait an hour for
That engine to come back.

The rails were oh, so shiny then—
So many trains went by.
I'd walk the rails on my way home—
A good trick, if you try.

And every night, when I was young,
I'd go to bed and know
That in the dead of night I'd hear
That lonesome whistle blow.